Close the
Achievement Gap:

Simple Strategies that Work

Brian M. Pete and Robin J. Fogarty

Close the Achievement Gap: Simple Strategies that Work

Published by Robin Fogarty & Associates, Ltd.
Chicago IL Santa Fe NM
800.213.9246
robin@robinfogarty.com
brian@robinfogarty.com
http://www.robinfogarty.com

Publisher: Brian Pete
Executive Editor: Robin Fogarty
Book Layout Design: Susana Siew Demunck
Cover Design: Susana Siew-Demunck
Editor: Mary Masters
Proofreader: Mary Masters
Production Coordinator: Tim Scott
Series Coordinator: Maple Ann Cervo

Printed in Australia

HAWKER BROWNLOW
•
E D U C A T I O N

ISBN 0-9747416-5-5

11 10 09 08 07 06 05 04   10 9 8 7 6 5 4 3 2 1

Acknowledgements

Global thinkers ...

Ron Edmonds re-evaluates the Coleman Report ... "It is possible!"

Larry Bell delineates six strategies to close the achievement gap.

Eleanor Renee Rodriquez challenges teachers: "What is it about me you can't teach?"

Ruby Payne presents the children of poverty in meaningful and memorable ways.

Katie Haycock advocates the right of children to quality teachers in every classroom.

Global producers ...

Hawker Brownlow Education publishes a teacher's library of resources.

Mary Masters edits with a fine eye for the written word.

Susana Siew-Demunck designs with the expert hand of the skilled artist.

Dedication

Tiffany Fegley Krubert

Teacher

Pritzker Elementary School

Chicago Public Schools

A teacher of such energy,

such caring and such passion ...

She is the inspiration for both authors,

(one a teacher, the other a student)

for the creation of this book.

Contents

Chapter 3

Chapter 4

Chapter 5

Introductory Comments: Head Start

The little girl on the cover of this book is Tatyana, three years old and home from her first day at Jackson-Steele Head Start in Hayneville, AL. For 40 years, Head Start has improved the lives of millions of children, supported the families of those most in need and reinforced the foundation of literacy in this great society. For people who know Head Start, it all comes back to children like Tatyana, little children just starting out, with big dreams and smiling faces.

This is about one of those faces. This is Tatyana's story.

Tatyana, at age three, was the center of attention at home. She made relatives laugh when she mimicked their voices, and she was bright and inquisitive. Tatyana's grandmother, Glissean Crittenden, has been teaching school for twenty-three years and is Tatyana's primary care giver. She got Tatyana up and ready for her first day at Head Start, braided her hair and attached the yellow and white daisy clips. Most of the children at Jackson-Steele Head Start ride the bus to school, a rural part of Lowndes County, one mile from the Freedom Trail, Selma to Montgomery, Alabama.

Tatyana's grandmother believed that Tatyana would do well in school. Yet she knows that Head Start has given Tatyana a significant boost toward a successful start in school. Tatyana's Head Start experience parallels the success strategies of quality teaching presented in this little book:

- Setting high expectations
- Challenging students to think
- Requiring rigor
- Leaving nothing to chance
- Making no excuses
- Insisting on results

Tatyana's teacher, Mrs Pringle, has high expectations. Tatyana learns responsibility through the daily procedures that every child is taught. She learns to put her bags away, to get her own supplies, and clean up after herself. Through the rituals, Tatyana learns discipline that carries over to the way she takes care of her own room at home.

Her school activities challenge her to think. Coloring with crayons involves matching colors to numbers; playing with toys means she learns the right sequence: chicken, egg, nest. Tatyana meets each new challenge and she even has fun with the difficult ones. She loves showing how smart she is.

A child, at age three, in a rural Alabama schoolhouse, may tend to get off task, and Tatyana is no different. But in her class, students are expected to meet the rigorous standards. The rigor that comes when teachers make sure that every student says, "Good morning," "Please," and "Thank you," and that every child speaks properly, using complete sentences and formal English.

There are three adults in Tatyana's class, two teachers and an aide. The class works in three groups, rotating from one instructor to the next, each teacher revisiting and re-teaching, leaving nothing to chance. The children know that they will be asked to repeat and recite what they are supposed to know.

In small groups every child gets a chance to show what they have learned. They are taught to take turns, to hold their hand up when they have an answer, and to wait for the teacher to call on them. They talk and share and care about one another. Tatyana sits next to a little girl who follows whatever Tatyana does, reading along with her, pointing to what she points at and sitting the way Tatyana sits. Every child counts in Head Start and every child has a collaborative environment of friends.

All the children in Jackson-Steele Head Start build literacy skills by working on phonics and letter recognition. They cut pictures from magazines and make sentences and tell stories. Tatyana learned the alphabet in her first year and you could hear her reciting it to herself all summer long as she played with her friends.

She is almost finished with her second year of Head Start and then it is on to kindergarten. Tatyana is just one of the faces of Head Start, yet through her story we know why Head Start is an important and effective way for children to begin their schooling. Because of it, she definitely has had a head start!

Introduction
Close the Achievement Gap: Simple Strategies that Work

Introductory Comments

There comes a time in a man's life when he realizes a purpose that is far greater than any he has been presented with before—a purpose that serves more than his material needs, more than the needs of his family, his community, or his own physical well-being. This purpose becomes clear on a spiritual level. It does not serve a need but shows itself as a moral imperative, clearly defined. This book is such an imperative.

It is impossible to paint the picture of impoverished children with a single brush full of one color from society's palette. Impoverished children come from the poorest circumstances anyone can imagine. They come from the urban centers of our cities where the ghettos form visible boundaries that skirt around the cities' exterior edges. They come from the country, hidden away in the hollows of mountainous terrain and the expanse of wide-open prairies. Children of poverty come from the reservations spotted in the high desert land and from the rugged landscapes of the tundra.

Poverty is the root cause of their circumstances; and, more importantly, poverty creates a debilitating mindset that affects the survival and the success of these unfortunate children. Poverty creates a mindset about the innate abilities, the background experiences, and the apparent willingness of these children to learn.

Poverty creates a debilitating mindset.

This mindset is so firmly in place, it is next to impossible to change it. In fact, the hardest hurdle to overcome in educating the children of poverty is this unshakable belief that they are not as capable as children born to more advantageous circumstances.

In a sentence, teachers, parents, and even the students themselves have low expectations for academic success. Teachers don't teach these kids as much, parents don't attend to their schooling as much, and students don't strive to achieve as much. And, in the end, as outrageous as it may sound, these low expectations become a self-fulfilling prophecy.

These data on the achievement gap tell part of this story of low expectations and the children of poverty in the discussion that follows. Yet, even with these data clearly stated, the fact is that all students can achieve, will achieve, and should prove these data wrong in schools of quality.

Society must come to believe that it is possible for all students to achieve, for, when a given population decides it is possible, it truly is. Children not only learn, children not only survive, but children thrive in these settings of high expectations, no excuses, and rigorous academic environments.

Achievement Gap Facts

Facts Defining the Achievement Gap

- There is a 30% illiteracy rate across American schools. Source: Joyce, 1999, p. 129.

- Only 1 in 50 Latino and 1 in 100 African American 17-year-olds can read and gain information from specialized text, such as the science section in the newspaper. Source: Haycock, 2001, p. 7.

- The fourth-grade reading slump is a myth. It's a slow decline, getting farther behind. Source: Barbara Taylor, personal communication, 12 July 2003.

- Students entering high school in the 35 largest cities in the United States read at the sixth-grade level. Students not reading at grade level are included in the achievement gap. Source: Vacca, 2002, p. 9.

- Achievement on literacy hasn't risen for 70 years. Source: Joyce, 1999, p. 129.

- U.S. students: the longer they are in school, the farther they fall behind the averages of other countries. Source: Joyce, 1999, p. 129.

- 90 million Americans lack basic literacy skills, with consequences for poverty, welfare, employment status, and crime. Source: U.S. Department of Education, 1993.

- Thirty-two states and the District of Columbia still do not release test scores by subgroups. Knowing the large gap separating students from different subgroups will be a call to action for educators. Source: Gehring, 2002, p. 2.

- Speaking is the number one skill for getting a job. Reading, writing, listening, and speaking skills are needed in the work place. Speaking is often overlooked and is critical for job interviews.

- 80% of the boys in middle school prefer non-fiction. Source: Barbara Taylor, personal communication, 12 July 2003.

- The only behavior measure that correlated significantly with reading scores is the number of books in the home; 61% of low-income families have no books at all in their homes. Source: U.S. Department of Education, retrieved April 24, 2003 from www.firstbook.org/about/factsonliteracy.html

Effects of the Achievement Gap

- Parents with professional jobs speak about 2,153 words an hour to their toddlers; those in poverty only about 616. A five-year-old child from a low-income home knows 5,000 words, while a middle-class child already knows 20,000 words. Source: Hart and Risley, 2003.

40% of all mathematics errors on state tests are reading errors.

- 40% of all mathematics errors on state tests are reading errors. Source: Joyce, 1999, p. 129.

- There is no sixth grade math test … it's cumulative; it's is a 6, 5, 4, 3, 2, 1 test. Source: Barbara Taylor, personal communication, 12 July 2003.

- Reading: Elementary School: 90% narrative text; High School, 90% informational text. The change in the type of reading affects the students' scores. Source: Barbara Taylor, personal communication, 12 July 2003.

- Informational text for Grade 1: 3% of reading (2.6 min./day); in Grades 2 to 5, 19% of reading. The amount of time spent reading informational text impacts student achievement. Source: Taylor, Pearson, Peterson, and Rodriguez, in press.

- A high school chemistry text can include 3,000 new vocabulary terms—more words than students are expected to learn in foreign language classes. Reading science texts requires additional reading skills that students may not have used in other content areas. Source: Barton, Heidema, and Jordan, 2002, p. 25.

- Algebra II is the new civil right. It's the threshold course. It more than doubles the odds that a student who enters postsecondary education will complete a bachelor's degree. The achievement gap will continue to grow unless more minority students participate in Algebra II courses. Source: Carnavale, 2003, p. 14.

- American businesses lose $60 million a year due to lack of employees' basic reading skills. Source: U.S. Department of Education, retrieved April 24, 2003 from www.firstbook.org/about/factsonliteracy.html

- 50% of high school dropouts are unemployed. Source: Schmoker, 1999b, p. 4.

- 68% of all prisoners are high school dropouts. Source: Schmoker, 1999b, p. 3.

- The State of Indiana bases projections for future prisons on number of second graders not reading at grade level. Source: Schmoker, 1999b, p. 4.

Evidence of Closing the Achievement Gap

- Literacy is vital to all subjects. Reciprocally, all subjects can enhance literacy. Source: Joyce, 1999, p. 129.

- Milwaukee Public Schools: 90% minority, 90% disadvantaged, but 90% at or above national norms in reading and mathematics. Source: Schmoker, 1999b, p. 1.

- Noticeable effects from 25 to 30 minutes of independent reading every day. The more time students spend independently reading, the greater the positive effect on student achievement. Source: Taylor, Pearson, Peterson, and Rodriguez, in press.

- Ten years ago, Kentucky was the first state to embrace standards-based reform. In reading, 7 of the 20 top-performing elementary schools are high-poverty schools. Source: Haycock, 2001, p. 4.

- What schools do matters enormously. And what matters most is good teaching, not, as previously believed. At one time the prevailing belief was that students' family income or parental educations outweighed the influence of teachers and schooling. Source: Haycock, 2001, p. 6.

- High student achievement correlates very strongly with strong administrative leadership, high expectations for student achievement, an orderly atmosphere conducive to learning, an emphasis on basic skill acquisition, and frequent monitoring of student progress. Source: Cawelti, 2003, p. 19, summarizing R. Edmond's work.

A Story: *Through the Cracks*

A striking image of the children "falling through the cracks" of our school systems is presented in the picture book *Through the Cracks*, by Sollman. While its scope is broader than what is traditionally perceived as "the achievement gap," the illustrations help educators visualize what happens with kids caught in the "achievement gap;" they have all the odds against them as far as school success.

Although, according to Carter, (*Ed Week*, 2004) "... the achievement gap consists of a complex set of problems (including disparities in graduation rates, school achievement, participation in higher education ...)," the picture depicts the kids who, for whatever reasons, aren't successful in, and often don't make it through, the schooling process. It makes the challenge real for those tackling the complexities of the closing the achievement gap.

The Mathew Effect

The Challenge of the Mathew Effect and the Achievement Gap

From the time kids enter school until about the time they exit third grade, even if they are falling behind, there is usually lots of help, with various materials available for many levels of readiness. The major focus of schooling in these early grades is on the many dimensions of literacy— listening, speaking, reading, and emergent writing. In addition to this strong literacy focus from the teacher and the curriculum, kids at this age can often fake it pretty well. They can get the 'gist' of the reading from the pictures, from the teacher's questions, and from the answers others say.

For these kids who are behind, after third grade, the gap just continues to widen.

However, once they pass beyond third grade, if they are significantly behind in their literacy skills, it becomes more and more difficult to catch up. In fact, there is a documented phenomenon called that Mathew Effect (Stanovitch, 1986). Named after the Book of Mathew in the Bible, the Mathew Effect basically notes that for these kids who are behind, after third grade, the gap just continues to widen. It seldom narrows and subsequently, they just keep getting farther and farther behind. Often, they give up on school entirely and physically drop out, or they continue slogging along, with no real hope of ever really making it in school.

That's why it is imperative that early literacy be a priority in our school programs. Yet, what about the ones beyond third grade who are still struggling? How do we address their needs? How do we intervene, to close the gap, before it widens any farther?

The Field Trip

There is another story about the achievement gap that warrants telling. It was told by teacher to her colleagues as they were studying their achievement data and becoming frustrated about what they could do to turn things around. They started complaining about all the time testing was taking from their teaching time, when this veteran teacher exclaimed, "It's like taking the kids on a field trip to the museum. You are constantly checking to see if all the kids are there; if they are with you and the rest of the group. If someone gets lost, if a group goes missing along the way, you don't wait until the end of the trip to go find them and get them back on track. You stop immediately and look for them. You assess the situation periodically, so you don't have a catastrophe at the end. That's what test results show us, and that's the purpose of looking at all this data. We want to know the facts about the achievement gap as we go, when there is time and opportunity to 'fix' it. Once we know who's where, and what's what, we can put our heads together and do something about it."

Heads Together

The last story involves a statement Mike Schmoker made at an educational conference. Walking by the open door of his presentation room, he was heard saying, "The most powerful school improvement tool we have is when teachers put their heads together, identify a concern, and brainstorm solutions to the problem. They are the ones closest to the problem. Therefore, they understand best the achievement concerns of their students and as experienced colleagues, who better to find the instructional intervention that has the most promise of turning things around."

> "The most powerful school improvement tool we have is when teachers put their heads together, identify a concern, and brainstorm solutions to the problem. They are the ones closest to the problem."

To elaborate on the statement that was overheard in the hallway, Schmoker goes on to say that there are three elements to this school improvement process: meaningful teams of teachers working together, managed data to inform the decisions, and measurable goals that are results oriented. Based on this simple model, school teams can have an impact on the achievement gap as we know it. Once the data is clear, the intervention must be carefully explored and then consistently, continually, and consciously implemented by all concerned.

Six Simple Strategies to Close the Achievement Gap

"Change is what teachers do and think. It's as simple and as complex as that." (Sarasan, in Fullan, 1999)

Katie Haycock, Director of the Education Trust, in Washington, DC, displays compelling data on her web site, www.edtruct.org. In that data, viewers see evidence of low performing schools turning around. Sometimes called the "90/90/90" schools (Reeves, 2003) because they are 90% low socio-economic, 90% minority, and 90% of students meet or exceed state/national norms in reading and math achievement, these schools prove the point that teachers can make the difference. All kids can learn. Edmonds (1982) was right! Teachers can overcome the impact of low socio-economic conditions. They can overcome the odds and guide these children to success.

Haycock goes on to delineate how these low performing schools improved so radically and she attributes the shift to quality teaching. To Haycock, and others (Stronge, 2002; Marzano, 2001; Schmoker, 1996), teacher quality is defined in no uncertain terms. In brief, Haycock summarizes quality teaching in this way. She says quality teachers have high expectations for all students, challenge students to think, require rigor in the classroom, make no excuses, leave nothing to chance, and insist on results-oriented goals.

As depicted in Figure 1, the six characteristics are succinct and strong. Quality teachers entertain high expectations for all students, not just for the students that "buy into the school game." These dedicated teachers challenge kids to think; to predict, to hypothesize, to infer;

to analyze, evaluate, and critique. The quality teachers in these low performing classrooms require rigor in all things. They require students to speak with skill and grace, write with clarity and purpose, read with a critical eye, and listen with active engagement.

> **These dedicated teachers challenge kids to think; to predict, to hypothesize, to infer; to analyze, evaluate, and critique.**

These quality teachers make no excuses; they accept no excuses. It's quite simple. They believe that all children can and will learn; all children can and will succeed. The teachers in these classrooms leave nothing to chance. Differentiation is part and parcel of everything they do. They ensure myriad entry points to learning by tapping into the multiple intelligence profile of each student. And last, but certainly not least, quality teachers insist on setting results-oriented goals for their classes. They count on positive results and they count what counts. They assess! They measure everything! They are accountable for increased student achievement.

---

1. Set high expectations for all students.

2. Challenge students to think.

3. Require rigor in the classroom.

4. Make no excuses.

5. Leave nothing to chance.

6. Insist on results.

Figure 1 Quality Teacher

It is these six characteristics that frame the ideas in this book. Married to an accompanying statement adapted from the work of Bell (2002), each of the six characteristics comprises a chapter. Each chapter includes a telling quote; a thorough description of characteristics, with cited researchers and voices in the field; a number of practical strategies that demonstrate what quality teachers say and do to implement the findings; reflections on the power of the characteristic; and films, books, and resources that support the identified behavior.

Chapter 1
Set High Expectations: Get Kids Emotionally Involved

"What are the reasons for the achievement gap?

The teachers say: 'Not enough books. No parent support. No time. Too many kids. The wrong kids. Poor facilities. The kids are tardy, undisciplined, and unable or unwilling to learn. It's not possible to turn things around.'

Kids say: 'They don't teach us as much as they teach the smart kids in the smart school.'"

Fogarty

Setting high expectations sounds like a simple order of the day. It's so easy to say "I expect all kids to do their best at all times." It's so easy to mean what you say. After all, what teacher does not expect all kids to learn? Yet, time-tested, nationally respected research, known as Teacher Expectations, Student Achievement (TESA) presents compelling evidence that teachers really don't have the same high expectations for all students (Kerman, 1982). In fact, there is a set of specific behaviors that teachers typically demonstrate that suggest just the opposite, that teachers have very different expectations for different kids.

Among the demonstrated behaviors are simple things:

1) Not distributing questions equally among all students; rather, asking questions more frequently of the students considered more able.

2) Not waiting as long for a student response with certain students considered less able.

3) Lack of teacher mobility in the classroom to ensure participation by all students.

In all, Kerman identifies 15 teacher behaviors in the TESA studies that suggest low expectations for developing students and higher expectations for others. The TESA behaviors are cited below in Figure 2.

1. Equitable Distribution of Response Opportunity

2. Affirmation or Correction

3. Proximity

4. Individual Helping

5. Praise for the Learning Performance

6. Courtesy

7. Latency

8. Reasons for Praise

9. Personal Interest Statements and Compliments

10. Delving, Rephrasing, Giving Clues

11. Listening

12. Touching

13. Higher-Level Questioning

14. Accepting Feelings

15. Desisting

Figure 2 TESA: Teacher Expectations, Student Achievement

TESA behaviors are described more fully later in this section on setting high expectations for all students, because this piece of research is so solid. TESA strategies, developed by the Los Angeles County Board of Education, CA, are still taught regularly in professional learning sessions across the country.

According to Katie Haycock, Director of Education Trust, a children's advocacy group in Washington, DC, when teachers have high expectations for all students, they don't just talk the talk; rather, they walk the talk. Teachers who believe that all children can, and, more importantly, will achieve, celebrate the diversity, the differences, and the uniqueness of every child. They focus on children first and content second. These highly effective teachers know that their students will care about what they know as teachers only after they know how much the teachers care about them as people.

They focus on children first and content second.

Haycock presents evidence of the power of the teacher as the number one determinant in the classroom of student success. She plainly states, "When you put highly qualified and quality-minded teachers into low performing classrooms the test scores go up and achievement increases." She goes on with a listing of characteristics that set these teachers apart from less effective teachers, which are examined later in this discussion. Yet, above all else, Kerman (1982), Haycock (2001), Marzano (2001), Schmoker (1996), Reeves (2001), Stronge, (2002), and others target high expectations as the critical element in the success of these disadvantaged, and often disenfranchised, students in these schools that have an unending history of failure.

Interestingly, Marzano and others make it crystal clear that the most difficult part of this scenario of low performing schools is not in teacher quality per se, as that can be changed quite significantly through professional development, but in the elusive task of convincing teachers that they can, in fact, make the difference. Teachers, according to Lortie (1975), are a caring lot. They want kids to do well.

It lies in the elusive task of convincing teachers that they can, in fact, make the difference.

To that end, teachers employ all kinds of strategies to enable students to succeed. Unfortunately, one of the most prevalent strategies inadvertently strikes this area of teacher expectations. Meaning well, teachers gently lower the requirements for these perceived "low performing kids." Teachers, in essence, "dummy down" the lesson or the curriculum in order to "help" the low kids.

While they have the best of intentions, there are unintended messages that accompany this strategy of lowering the bar. The most significant of these unintended messages seems subtle, yet it is sent to these kids so loud, it may as well have been shouted from the rooftops: "You are not as smart as some of the other kids, so I'm not going expect as much from you. I care about you, but I think you are dumb."

Now, this may sound a bit harsh, in the light of the current academic focus on differentiating learning to reach and teach all students, yet, the kids do not miss the unintended message. Nothing escapes these school-weary, struggling learners, and they know in their hearts that they have a "label."

How do teachers come to believe in high expectations as the right of every child in their care? How do they come to understand the hidden messages that are sent when they innocently harbor lower expectations for some? How do caring and skillful teachers act upon high expectations, and what are the instructional protocols that speak to high expectations in the classroom?

With a plethora of research that speaks to the issues embedded in the complexities of holding high expectations, there are a number of explicit strategies teachers can implement as they become more aware and more attentive to the impact of high expectations. Some of these strategies are evident in the TESA behaviors: be more mobile during the lesson; employ a gimmick, such as a fishbowl of student names, to ensure all kids are called upon; or use the strategy of "wait time" (3–5 second pause after asking a questions). Others are more involved, such as incorporating knowledge of emotional intelligence into classroom activities in order to get students on board emotionally for optimal learning.

Strategies

Perhaps the most powerful strategy to set high expectations for all students is captured in the concept of emotional involvement. When teachers elicit student buy-in (student engagement in the activities, student investment in the learning, student ownership of a project) teachers set the bar for all of the kids. In essence, teachers who understand the connection between emotions and cognition (Caine, 1991) are the teachers who understand that all kids want to learn, all kids can learn, and all kids will learn, in their classroom.

Perhaps the most powerful strategy to set high expectations for all students is captured in the concept of emotional involvement.

Twelve Brain Principles

Renate and Geoffrey Caine (1991) founded a set of twelve principles that apply to the human brain and learning. Through a meta-analysis methodology, in a seminal book called *Making Connections: Teaching and the Human Brain*, they exposed these twelve principles that govern instructional decision-making. These twelve principles are illustrated below in Figure 3.

Principle #1:	Challenge engages the brain, threat inhibits it.
Principle #2:	Emotions and cognition are linked.
Principle #3:	Learning involves both focused and peripheral attention.
Principle #4:	The brain learns through parts and wholes simultaneously.
Principle #5:	There are two types of memory systems: implicit and explicit.
Principle #6:	The brain is a parallel processor.
Principle #7:	Learning involves the entire physiology.
Principle #8:	Each brain is unique.
Principle #9:	Learning is embedded in experience.
Principle #10:	The search for meaning is innate.
Principle #11:	The search for meaning occurs through patterning.
Principle #12:	Learning always involves unconscious and conscious processing.

Figure 3 Twelve Brain Principles

Principle #1: Challenge Engages the Brain, Threat Inhibits It

This principle makes the case for differentiation in terms of learner readiness. In creating standards-based curriculum units, teachers can include tiered activities that challenge, but don't threaten different levels of learners.

Principle #2: Emotions and Cognition are Linked

Emotional involvement gets the brain's attention and guides differentiation. Once the learner is attentive, short-term memory kicks in and memory is the only evidence we have of learning. When planning curriculum units, teachers include a variety of activities that tap into the emotions of the youngsters. Differentiation is inherent, as some kids are motivated by one thing and other kids are motivated by another.

Principle #3: Learning Involves both Focused and Peripheral Attention

As teachers develop units of study around the standards, they design activities to purposefully target the goals of the curriculum. But, teachers also differentiate the curriculum unknowingly, as students take away different learnings. For example, all of the kids may understand how to find the circumference of a circle, yet some kids also learn incidentally how to work with a partner, or how to draw a perfect circle, or any number of other peripheral things. In fact, 70% of learning is peripheral, so teachers must value the entire process of developing the curriculum unit.

Principle #4: The Brain Learns Through Parts and Wholes Simultaneously

Interestingly, some students prefer to learn by starting with the big picture, while others prefer to start with the parts or skills or pieces. For example, one student looks at the whole decade that they are studying, while another wants to dig into one specific area such as the music of the era.

Both students will end up studying the entire unit, but they will emphasize different aspects.

Principle #5: There are Two Types of Memory Systems: Implicit and Explicit

Knowing that there are two types of memory systems, teachers can ensure that the curriculum is brain-based, as well as standards-based. This is done by incorporating explicit memory activities that require practice, repetition, and rehearsal, and at the same time, fostering implicit memory by building on authentic experiences. For example, some students may want to memorize the elements in the Periodic Table of Elements, while others learn best from the lab experiences, actually using the elements.

Principle #6: The Brain is a Parallel Processor

Developing curriculum that taps into all four lobes of the brain's neo-cortex helps differentiate curriculum. The four lobes include the frontal lobe (thinking), the occipital lobe (vision), the temporal lobe (auditory), and the parietal lobe (integration of the senses). Curriculum units that use many of the senses develop areas of visual activity as well as auditory experience and higher order thinking, and naturally differentiate by student strengths.

Principle #7: Learning Involves the Entire Physiology

Simply by being aware of the role of nutrition, exercise, and relaxation in learning, teachers can differentiate curriculum. For instance, they can weave movement into some of the unit activities and reflection into others. They can advocate nutritious meals and adequate sleep.

Principle #8: Each Brain is Unique

Probably one of the most relevant ways to differentiate curriculum is through the application of this principle. Each brain is unique, based on genetic codes (nature) and background experiences (nurture). With this understanding, teachers can design curriculum units with broad appeal to a wide range of learning profiles, abilities, and interests; include individual, small group, and whole group activities; include role plays and simulations, music, and the visual and performing arts; include reading, writing, speaking, and listening activities, and tap into the many kinds of minds represented in that classroom.

Principle #9: Learning is Embedded in Experience

Most teachers understand the value of giving kids the real experience, rather than a representation of the experience. Taking the kids to the zoo will always have more powerful learning impact than simply reading about the zoo. When youngsters come to school lacking in experiences, teachers must try to create the experiences in creative ways. Naturally, each learner takes away a different impression of the moment, but that is exactly how robust curriculum models differentiate.

Principle #10: The Search for Meaning is Innate

When teachers utilize investigations and inquiry models of curriculum, student curiosity, interests, and readiness levels help determine the investigative path each learner takes. Puzzles, conundrums, moral dilemmas, and real world problems are appropriate curriculum tools.

Principle #11: The Search for Meaning Occurs Through Patterning

Using themes, principles, rules, theorems, big ideas, and concepts are all ways to help differentiate the curriculum. Students need that perspective, that context, in order to make sense of things and fit the new material into their individual existing schema. That is differentiation at its best.

Principle #12: Learning Always Involves Unconscious and Conscious Processing

The idea that learning continues even after the formal lesson, throughout the unit of study, and even into the next units, is a call for a more connected and coherent curriculum. Differentiation is infused into curriculum units when there is time for reflection and connection making. Again, each makes his/her own connections, but in the end, they all have an understanding of the information.

Student Choice

Whenever possible, provide the opportunity for students to choose what they will read, how they will write about it, when they will have it completed, and how much help they need from you. When the teachers hook kids into the learning by giving them options and choices about their learning, their actions speak louder than any words they could possibly say. What student choice says to these kids is: "I believe in you. I believe you can make good decisions about your own learning. I trust you and I trust your judgments."

Teacher Expectations, Student Achievement – TESA Behaviors (Kerman, 1982)

1. Equitable Distribution of Response Opportunity

Using strategies that guarantee all students equal opportunity to respond or perform in classroom situations, such as using a set of name cards for a regular rotation for calling upon students.

2. Affirmation or Correction

Using feedback strategies to give students comments about their performance.

3. Proximity

Being mobile in the classroom and being physically close to various students at various times.

4. Individual Helping

Guiding the process and mediating the learning by giving students the specific help they need.

5. Praise for the Learning Performance

Using praise appropriately for student learning performances.

6. Courtesy

Using expressions of courtesy and kindness with students to set a safe and caring learning environment.

7. Latency

Using wait-time strategies—a 3–5 second pause following a teacher-generated question—to allow time for kids to think before they respond.

8. Reasons for Praise

Using appropriate praise that is specific, timely, and well-grounded.

9. Personal Interest Statements and Compliments

Asking appropriate questions, giving compliments, and making statements related to students' personal interests.

10. Delving, Rephrasing, Giving Clues

Using additional information, asking a second question, rephrasing an initial question, cueing, and prompting students to respond.

11. Listening

Applying active and attentive listening techniques with students; using paraphrasing, affirmations, clarifying questions, and eliciting deeper, elaborated responses.

12. Touching

Supporting student responses in a friendly manner, with appropriate, respectful, and meaningful touching behaviors, such a putting a gentle hand on the shoulder of a student to encourage him as he struggles with a response.

13. Higher-Level Questioning

Asking higher-level questions that require mindful answers of analysis, synthesis, or evaluation.

14. Accepting Feelings

Accepting student feelings in a non-evaluative manner; recognizing the emotions and feelings of students in learning situations.

15. Desisting

Using calm and courteous techniques to intervene with disruptive student behaviors; not allowing the disruption to escalate, but rather helping to de-escalate the situation.

Facing the Day with Feelings

Have kids draw three faces: one to show how they felt yesterday, another that shows how they feel today, and a third that shows how they predict they will feel tomorrow.

The Right Way

Working in AB pairs, have A tell a story about a time when s/he was so angry that just thinking about it brings the angry feelings back again. Then, have B ask several questions to determine if A demonstrated his/her anger the right way.

Were you angry at the right person?
To the right degree?
At the right time?
With the right action?
About the right thing?

Debrief on the power of teaching kids about how to deal with their feelings and how to evaluate their behaviors when certain feelings occur.

Reflections

What Teachers Make

The dinner guests were sitting around the table discussing life, jobs, salaries, and such. One guest asked, "You're a teacher, Susan. Be honest. What do you make?"

Susan, who had a reputation of honesty and frankness, replied, "You want to know what I make?"

"I make kids work harder than they ever thought they could."
"I make kids wonder."
"I make them question."
"I make them apologize and mean it."

"I make them write."
"I make them read, and read, and read."
"I make kids sit through 40 minutes of study hall in absolute silence."

"I make them spell, 'definitely beautiful' over and over and over again, until they will never misspell either one of those words, ever again."

"I make kids show all their work in math and hide it all on their final drafts in English."

"I make them understand that if they have brains, they will follow their hearts … and if someone ever tries to judge them by what they make, they should pay no attention."

"You know what I make? "
"I make a difference."

"What about you?"

Anonymous

Film

Dead Poets Society

Use the clip from *Dead Poets Society* (1989) when the teacher, played by Robin Williams, has the students ripping the pages from the literature text. He asks them to think about meaning of life and what the future holds for them, and he asks them, with all the passion of a poet, "What will your verse be?"

Chapter 2
Challenge Students to Think: Teach Higher Order Thinking

"Make kids think. Challenge them. Allow them struggle. Give them the gift of a sense of accomplishment."

Fogarty

Teachers are caring individuals. They want their students to succeed. They will do whatever they can to help their students pass their class. In fact, in their well-intentioned way, teachers may even "spoon feed" their students to make sure they "get it" and that they get it right. For example, teachers may assign a research paper to experienced high school students, and then persist in scaffolding the process for these seniors as though they were inexperienced newcomers. They tell them when and how to do their research, their notes, their outline, and their finished piece.

Yet, in the best interests of the students, teachers need to challenge them to think, to reason, and to make sense of things in their own minds. Teachers need to trust the learners; to permit the learners to feel the anxiety of plotting, planning, and executing an entire project. In fact, kids need to be encouraged to make their own decisions and to live with those decisions; to make the needed adjustments to succeed, yet to know that they are in charge of their own thinking and their own work.

> **Teachers need to challenge them to think, to reason, and to make sense of things in their own minds.**

Now, that doesn't mean that the teacher is not there to guide the process when necessary, when asked, or when an impending crisis indicates some intervention might be needed, but students do need to feel the tenseness of not knowing, of wondering about an authentic problem that has many dimensions. Students need to experience the discomfort of ambiguous situations. They need to practice making meaning in their minds; making critical connections that seem logical and reasonable. Students need to feel like they are capable of the task; that they are able to manage their own learning. They need to know that they can rely on their own resources and their power to think through a situation.

As Piaget (1954) has shown, learners make meaning in their minds. They construct meaning by connecting new information and incoming data to prior knowledge and background experiences. The learner must make the critical connections in order to make sense of the world around him or her. That's the constructivist theory of learning.

In addition, Vygotsky's (1978) view comes into play as one explores this idea of challenging students to think. Vygotsky believes that as students construct meaning in their minds, they do it through a social setting; in discussion with others. As the learner thinks deeply about an idea, her dialogue with another helps her clarify her own thinking. This kind of conversation causes the learner to examine his or her thinking more acutely and thus, concepts are formed and real understanding begins to occur. Again, it is the challenge to let kids think that is at the heart of the construction of meaning.

However, the role of the teacher is critical as kids learn to think; as they learn to predict and infer; to compare and to contrast; as they determine cause and effect; or as they analyze, evaluate and critique. This is when the teacher is truly the guide or the mediator of learning. According to Feuerstein (1980), this is when the teacher prompts the thinking with cueing questions or challenges the thinking with an opposing view. This is the true picture of a mindful classroom, in which students are challenged to think, challenged to question their own thinking, and challenged to question the thinking of others before them.

Harkening back to the first premise about expectations, when teachers truly harbor high expectations for all kids, they fuel those expectations with challenges in the learning environment that force kids gently into the rigors and the richness of higher order thinking. Teachers who truly believe in kids, in the innate ability of all kids to think, in the untapped talents of all kids to become all they are capable of becoming, in the inherent resources of each and every one of their students; these are the teachers who help their kids soar, because these wise teachers know that their kids can and will think if they are expected to think and if they are explicitly taught the skills of thinking.

> **Because these wise teachers know that their kid can and will think if they are expected to think.**

To teach the skills of higher order thinking, there are two kinds of thinking that teachers target. One involves the analytical skills of critical thinking and the other encompasses the generative skill of creative thinking. Within the realm of critical thinking, students learn how to take things apart, analyze, evaluate, compare/contrast, classify, find similarities and differences, and use metaphors and analogies. As students practice their creative thinking, they learn to use productive thinking skills that include hypothesizing, predicting, making inferences, creating generalizations, visualizing, and going beyond the obvious. These are the thinking skills of an intellectual life and of authentic life of unending challenges.

A wonderful compendium of these necessary thinking skills is found in the best practices of Marzano, Pickering, and Pollock (2001). In their meta-analysis of instructional practices, they found a family of nine best practices that have profound impact on learning. The nine best practices appear below in Figure 4.

1	SD	Finding Similarities and Differences
2	SN	Summarizing and Note Taking
3	RR	Reinforcing Effort and Recognition
4	HP	Homework and Practice
5	NR	Nonlinguistic Representation
6	CL	Co-operative Learning
7	OF	Objectives and Feedback
8	GH	Generating Hypotheses
9	QCA	Questions, Cues, and Advance Organizers

Figure 4 Nine Best Practices

In the final analysis, as noted earlier in the Gap Facts section, literacy is at the root of the achievement gap. In turn, literacy—reading, writing, speaking, and listening—requires skillful thinking processes similar to those discussed in the beginning of this discussion. And, interestingly, many of these thinking skills are included in the nine best practices of Marzano, Pickering, and Pollock (2001), listed and described briefly in the following Strategies section of the chapter.

Strategies

Three-Story Intellect

The lines from the Oliver Wendell Holmes novel, *Poet at the Breakfast Table* (1939) begin,

"There are one story intellects, two story intellects and three story intellects with skylights. All fact collectors who have no aim beyond their facts, are one story minds. Two story minds, compare reason, generalize using the labor of the fact collectors as their own. Three story minds idealize, imagine, predict—their best illumination comes from above, through the skylight."

Working in three teams to illustrate the three stories of the intellect on large poster paper, teachers create a large segmented poster. They hang the Three-Story Intellect poster in the classroom for easy reference to higher order thinking. They ask kids occasionally, "Are we using our three-story intellects or are we on the ground floor?"

Fat and Skinny

Introduce the concepts of fat and skinny questions. Fat questions require lots of thinking and in-depth answers to fully explain a point of view or an opinion, whereas, skinny questions require a simple "Yes," "No," or "Maybe" answer so they get no real attention at all, and lead nowhere in terms of higher order thinking.

Use the metaphor of fat and skinny questions whenever students are working, writing, or thinking.

Unpack the Language

To help students understand the directions in work samples, in textbook chapters, and on the tests they continually take, let them unpack the language in the directions. Help them find the action words, the words that tell them what they are supposed to do, and then help them "unpack" the language in ways that they can understand. For example, help them unpack the directions, "What can you infer from this line?" by naming synonyms for the word infer: guess, conclude, think about, know, etc.

Threaded Model of Skill Development

Take any higher order thinking skill and thread it through the curriculum by threading the thinking skill into every subject area. Thread the idea of making inferences in PE by guessing what the opponent will do; make inferences in science by interpreting what the observations suggest; make inferences in math by predicting where the graph line will go; make inferences in social studies by speculating what parallels there are to current situations; and make inferences in art by drawing conclusions about the era.

Nine Best Practices

Each of nine best practices is briefly reviewed in the following list.

1 SD Finding Similarities and Differences

Comparing and contrasting, classifying, solving analogies, and the use of metaphors and similes.

2 SN Summarizing and Note Taking

The use of regular note taking, summarizing, synthesizing, and retelling.

3 RR Reinforcing Effort and Recognition

Commenting on effort and using methods to recognize individual students.

4 HP Homework and Practice

Rehearsal, repetition, and traditional homework assignments that are purposeful and meaningful.

5 NR Nonlinguistic Representation

Graphic organizers or visual tools used to sort information and make sense of things.

6 CL Co-operative Learning

Co-operative strategies and structures used for team activities.

7 OF Objectives and Feedback

Standards of learning, benchmarks, and goals with appropriate, frequent, and relevant feedback.

8 GH Generating Hypotheses

Making predictions, inferences, and educated guesses that go beyond the given information.

9 QCA Questions, Cues, and Advance Organizers

Cueing techniques that spark student thinking.

Reflections

While all teachers ultimately care deeply about all of their students, they don't all have the highest expectations for all of their students. As demonstrated in the TESA research (Kerman, 1982), well-intentioned teachers can signal through both verbal and non-verbal behaviors that they do not expect as much from some kids as they do from others. Sometimes, those levels of expectations are all too obvious to the students themselves. This dilemma of expectations, the profound impact of low expectations, is poignantly illustrated in the following poem in figure 5.

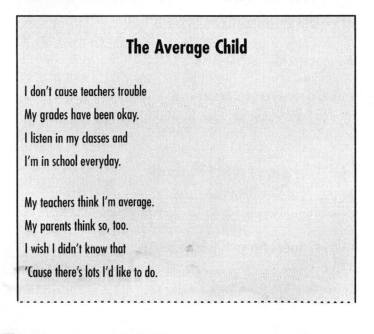

The Average Child

I don't cause teachers trouble
My grades have been okay.
I listen in my classes and
I'm in school everyday.

My teachers think I'm average.
My parents think so, too.
I wish I didn't know that
'Cause there's lots I'd like to do.

I would like to build a rocket
I have a book that tells you how
Or start a stamp collection.
Well, no use in trying now.

'Cause since I found I am average
I'm just smart enough, you see,
To know there's nothing special
That I should expect of me.

I am part of that majority,
That hump part of the bell,
Who spends his life unnoticed
In an average kind of hell.

    Anonymous

Figure 5 High Expectations for Every Child

Film Clip

Saturday Night Live: The Best of Jerry Seinfeld

Teachers can use the skit called, "World War II 101," in the videotape, *Saturday Night Live: The Best of Jerry Seinfeld* (1992). The tape presents a hysterically funny history teacher trying to get his students to think. "I want you to think, today. Let's all just think," is his lament to his earnest young high school class.

.

Chapter 3
Require Rigor: Require Complete Sentences, Standard English, Formal Register

"Good Morning, Class. I'm Miss Hobbs and I'm going to be your teacher. I love you kids and I'm always going to be here for you. But, I want you to know that in this class, we go to the deep water. We learn the hard stuff and we take some risks. But, don't worry. I'm going to give you the skills you need to survive and thrive, because I know you can."

Nelda Hobbs

Require rigor! Create an atmosphere of formality that students respect and adhere to. Don't lowball the learning. Effective teachers let kids know that things are going to be done right in their classrooms. They send the message loudly and clearly, that half-hearted, second-rate efforts are not acceptable. These teachers make it known that in their classrooms only first-rate work is acceptable. They set the bar high, model doing their best, and expect all students to give their all. They let it be known that they are there for the kids and that they expect the kids to be there for them ... fully, consistently, and without fail.

> **Effective teachers let kids know that things are going to be done right in their classrooms.**

These teachers require rigor in all aspects of student involvement: they require rigor in their attire and grooming; they require rigor in their attitude and demeanor; they require rigor in their speech and writing; they require rigor in their thinking and responses; and they require rigor in their products and performances. And, believe it or not, students want the bar set high. They want to know the parameters and they want to know that expectations are of the highest quality. Students like the idea of rigor and doing things that are hard. They especially like the idea of doing things with quality, because it means that the teacher believes that the students are able, willing, and capable of meeting the rigorous requirements.

Require Rigor in their Attire and Grooming

There's a scene in the movie, *To Sir, with Love*, in which the teacher, played by Sidney Poitier, sets the standards of dress for his outrageous class. He tells them that they are to dress appropriately for class or they will not be allowed into the room. In his own way, he is setting the standard for the idea of "dressing for success."

Some schools actually endorse a dress code by requiring a school uniform. While the idea of a dress code is not always embraced enthusiastically by parents, students, or teachers, many schools are moving toward some sort of requirements for student attire. For example, many middle schools and high schools have "outlawed" hats and caps of any kind, body piercings, head-sets, and cell phones. As part and parcel of this movement, schools have placed restrictions on T-shirts with outlandish messages; long, flowing trench coats; low-riding, hip-hugger jeans; and short, midriff tops that expose the skin.

With all this fuss about appropriate dress, it does seem that a rigorous dress code is a needed and sensible move. It seems to follow that when one is dressed with thoughtful care, they will probably act with that same degree of thoughtful care. In any case, effective teachers often set clear standards about what is acceptable and what will not be tolerated in terms of grooming and dress.

> **Effective teachers often set clear standards about what is acceptable and what will not be tolerated, in terms of grooming and dress.**

One middle school teacher shared her strategy of saving the various toiletries from hotel visits. She then used the items to stock her classroom closet with bars of soap, small bottles of shampoo, miniature containers of mouthwash, and various and sundry other supplies for her early adolescents. In her relationship with her class, she made it easy for them to care about good grooming and to respect the classroom situation enough to consider how they dressed. Rigor, once again, is the key concept for these teachers.

Require Rigor in their Attitude and Demeanor

When teachers demonstrate a positive approach to life and living, and when they model productive problem solving and sound decision-making, the message is subtly broadcast to their students. When teachers carry themselves with dignity, when they act with integrity, and when they are consistent, fair, and predictable in all their dealings, kids respond with similar attitudes and they strive to actually change their demeanor to reflect what they think the teacher wants. Students usually want to please the teacher, the authority figure in their world of school. They do respond to this kind of rigor in accepted behaviors.

Require Rigor in their Speech and Writing

Speaking in complete sentences is one of the easiest and most straightforward strategies that teachers employ.

> **By insisting on oral replies that are complete thoughts with syntax and semantics in place, the student is, in reality, rehearsing the verbal skills of a literate person.**

Requiring students to speak in complete sentences, as they interact spontaneously and as they respond more formally to questions and prompts from the teacher, sets high expectations for literacy skills. By insisting on oral replies that are complete thoughts with syntax and semantics in place, the student is, in reality, rehearsing the verbal skills of a literate person. Eventually, this oral language translates into the student's reading fluency and into their written language.

In low achieving schools, where factual recall is the level of instruction in many of the classrooms, students are rarely required to explain their thinking in complete sentences. Questions that are designed for one-word answers increase the likelihood that students will not practice or value speaking in ways that indicate higher levels of literacy.

As suggested earlier, speaking in complete sentences does lead to writing and reading in complete sentences. This kind of rigor adds challenge to the classroom, in an area where many students feel inadequate. If students are uncomfortable trying to explain their thoughts or their confusion in a lesson because of poor language skills, they quietly fall farther behind. On the other hand, writing is the other expressive language skill. Just as student speaking is a target for quality, so too is their written work.

Writing, by its very nature, is the more formal expression of what one says. In fact, when learning to write, teachers often say, "Write about what you know," implying that the things students know best, the things they talk about all the time, are the very things they are most likely to target in their writing. These are the things they know and care about. Therefore, they are the things to explore more fully and more formally through writing. Most writers would agree with this idea. They are known to remark that they tend to write about the things they have been talking about and attending to in their reading and in their conversations with colleagues.

Thus, when students are required to write as part of their work or as an assignment, effective teachers encourage students to write from their experiences and to write with the standard conventions of grammar, spelling, and punctuation. Teachers coach students through the first and second drafts and then set the bar for the final entry. They let students know through the use of checklists and/or scoring rubrics what the quality requirements are and what the quality indicators are.

Even in this situation, contrary to what some may think, students really do embrace the high standards. Once these kinds of stringent requirements are set forth and consistently and continually enforced, students rise to the rigor of high expectations and know that only quality work is acceptable.

Require Rigor in their Thinking and Responses

Again, by modeling, demonstrating, and calling attention to the rigors of good thinking, kids begin to mimic the behaviors and wind up reasoning their way through various situations that occur in the course of their class work. When teachers model logical, deductive thinking; when they label the inductive thinking skills of taking specific information and moving to concepts that can be generalized; when teachers respond thoughtfully to student queries and demonstrate their steps to solving problems; and when teachers are mindful and thoughtful in all their interactions, students adopt those very same behaviors. Teachers must not be afraid to require rigor. It is in the best interest of their young learners.

Teachers must not be afraid to require rigor. It is in the best interest of their young learners.

Require Rigor in their Products and Performances

Teachers must expect only the best, only the most quality product, only the most perfect performance. They must require students to reach for the stars, because in that most supreme effort, students reach maximum heights and that is what is expected in the world of family and work: to do your very best each and every time.

As the reader ponders this section, she may be tempted to say, "Oh, this is over the top. Kids can't always perform with such rigorous quality." Yet, they can, and they will, if that is what is expected. If teachers let their guard down, even for that one moment in time, the kids will be there to take advantage of the lapse. After all, that's what kids do. Yet, if the rigor is part and parcel of the classroom package, rigor will reign supreme.

Strategies

Down Memory Lane

There was a time in school when we all had to memorize a speech, a scene in a play or poem. This rote learning created a sense of accomplishment and helped us understand the patterns and cadence of proper speech. Share something that you had to memorize. What was the occasion? How did you do it? And, how did it feel to struggle and then to finally master the passage?

Diagramming Sentences

Diagramming sentences is an activity that has gone by the wayside in the average classroom. Diagramming sentences serves as a visual aid, like a graphic organizer, that different students may respond to because they are visual/spatial learners. Diagram a sentence and leave it on the board for the week. Work through the basic concepts of diagramming sentences. Pique the interests of the students to the complex construction of sentences and at the same time show them the value of taking things apart to understand them better.

Put Words in My Mouth

Put a different complete, complex sentence on the board each week and challenge your students to mimic the phrase, using their words, when making all requests for hall passes, extra help, etc. For example:

"I speak to you today, not as a lawyer, not as a man from Boston, not as a man from Massachusetts, but as an American."

Daniel Webster

"I ask you this morning, not as a fifth grader, not as a student from Howard Middle School, not as the son of Mabel McPherson, but as a young man who needs to go to the bathroom."

DeWayne McPherson

The Sentence Squad

Used consistently and persistently, the strategy of requiring students to speak and to write in complete sentences can have profound and lasting effects. While this sounds like such a simple strategy, it proves to be a somewhat troublesome strategy to enforce. The rapid pace of classroom questioning gets in the way of more precise, accurate, and complete responses. But, when teachers use the strategy as a game, the Sentence Squad students "police" each other for complete sentence usage at all times. In turn, the oral and written language of the students improves dramatically.

Mr. Pete's Questions

Teachers can use, Mr. Pete's Questions (Pete & Fogarty, 2004) to foster use of more robust responses (and the use of complete sentences) by prompting students' first response, which is usually a one-word answer, with the following cues:

1. "Tell me more about that."

2. "What else? What's another possible answer?"

3. "Give me an example of what you said."

Reflection

Mr. Parnes' Questions

Another strategy to promote full sentences and more comprehensive answers, is to ask two questions suggested by Parnes (1977), who believes if teachers ask these two questions they will propel learning to a higher level.

1. "How does this connect to something you already know?"

2. "How might you use this in the future?"

Teachers often use this as a reflective tool following an introductory lesson.

Film

To Sir, With Love

In this 1967 classic, Sidney Poitier requires a certain level of dress, language, and overall behavior (manners and etiquette) in his inner city classroom. He proclaims, "In this classroom, you will dress appropriately, use manners at all times, and speak in complete sentences. That is how the civilized society behaves." Teachers use this to raise the bar for routine courtesy and "civilized" interactions in the classroom. After viewing the video, students can set the "rules and regs" for their own classroom.

Chapter 4
Leave Nothing to Chance:
Revisit! Review! Re-teach! Revise!

"'I told them what they're supposed to know. Why don't they know it?'

Interestingly, just because teachers say something, just because they 'cover' it, doesn't mean the students have learned it."

Madeline Hunter

"Covering your content, completing the text, and addressing all of the content standards in your area, doesn't mean the kids learned it. In fact, covering your content is sort of like taking a passenger to the airport. You may get to the airport in time, but you left the passenger at home. When you finished the science text, did the kids come with you?"

To farther illustrate the idea of leaving nothing to chance, a principal tells this story:

> "I said to my staff, 'We've been using data to drive instructional decisions for seven years, yet, nothing has changed. Our test scores are virtually the same as they were seven years ago. My conclusions are, either we don't know how to teach reading and math or we don't know what the data is telling us.
>
> 'Now, let's look at these test scores, again, and tell the story of the data.'

As one teacher stood up, she said, almost in a whisper, 'What this data tells me is that the longer a kid is in our school, the worse he does.' And she broke into tears."

That was the turning point for this school. Now, when they look at the test data and examine the various sub-skills, they ask these critical questions, "When do we think we taught that skill? Did we revisit it? Did it spiral through the day, the week, the unit? How do we know the students know it? Let's leave nothing to chance. Let's revisit it! Let's make sure they know it in all its forms."

Great teachers leave nothing to chance. They don't assume every kid got it. They make sure every kid got it.

Great teachers leave nothing to chance.

They revisit! They review! They re-teach! They revise. They put as much focus on the learning as they do on the teaching. They know that it's not about them, it's about the students. It's not just about their teaching or their elegant, exquisite lesson. It's about the students and their individual learning. These teachers understand that there are two elements at work, one is teaching and the other is learning. Thus, they must revisit, review, re-teach, and revise.

Revisit – Routinely revisit (spiral) concepts/skills throughout day, week, unit

Review – Routinely review concepts/skills in robust ways

Re-teach – Routinely re-teach the concepts/skills with differentiation

Revise – Routinely revise concepts/skills; mediate, guide, and correct all
answers

Figure 6 Leave Nothing to Chance

Routinely Revisit

Great teachers routinely revisit new concepts and freshly introduced skills. They revisit frequently, briskly, continually, and in a variety of ways. They check for understanding, and when they don't get the level of assurance they need, they pull kids together for flexible skill groupings. These teachers know that once is not enough. Even eight is not enough. In fact, it might take up to twenty times for students to learn new skills and concepts. Revisiting recently introduced ideas, regularly and often, is integral to the teaching/learning process.

Revisiting an idea means spiraling the skill or concept throughout the day, the week, the unit. For example, the concept of fractions may be introduced in the morning math class, through an extensive lesson using manipulatives, drawings, and the actual symbolic representations of fractions. Then, the teacher might revisit the idea of fractions briskly and relevantly, before lunch, by suggesting students eat "half" a sandwich and then drink "half a container" of milk. It just takes this quick reference to the morning math concept to cycle it back into the minds of the students. They might even write the half symbol and just "play" with the idea.

Following lunch, the teacher may ask the class to divide in half, creating two teams for a social studies debate. Once again, the teacher is simply revisiting the idea of fractions in a meaningful way. In addition, the fraction takes on more meaning as it is applied to the class interaction. Finally, the teacher may revisit the concept of fractions one more time before the students leave for the day, by suggesting that they tell a partner one way they used fractions that day.

In a most meaningful way, teachers can revisit an idea through a meaningful, purposeful homework assignment in which students are using fractions in some way. Perhaps they are asked to review two recipes and notice the fractions. They may even be asked to bring their favorite recipe in to share.

> **In a most meaningful way, teachers can revisit an idea through a meaningful, purposeful homework assignment.**

According to Marzano, Pickering, and Pollock (2001), the research on doing one half hour of substantive homework can increase grades in that subject area by as much as one half the grade point average. That is compelling evidence to think about revisiting an idea through a mere half-hour of homework each night.

Routinely Review

Great teachers routinely review new concepts, skills and ideas. While revisiting an idea may take the form of a quick reference just to spark the mind, reviewing is a more substantial look at the lesson again. It is a 4–5 minute review that establishes the key thoughts, the steps, the stages, and phases of the content focus. Reviewing is a micro-look that refreshes the mind of the operations needed to complete the skill or to apply the concept.

An example of a lesson review is illustrated in a grammar lesson on parts of speech. While the students are initially introduced to the eight parts of speech (nouns, verbs, adjectives, adverbs, pronouns, prepositions, conjunctions, and interjections), review lessons in this context may elaborate on each one more fully. Students might review the entire list, and then the teacher zeros in on one part of speech and emphasizes it with farther explanations, examples, and elaborations.

A sample review lesson on parts of speech may have students name all eight and guess which one is the focus of the micro-lesson as the teacher shows the following words:

Dark, huge, square, tall, light, red, tiny, mysterious, heavy, funny, indescribable.

Then she says, "Adjectives are colorful words that modify the noun. They describe size, color, shape, height, weight, consistency, and type."

Micro-reviews are frequent, consistent, and continual as the initial introductory lesson is synthesized, analyzed, evaluated, illustrated, and generally unpacked for deeper understanding. These quick, focused reviews are integral to the introductory lesson. They extend the lesson for the student by adding specifics and details to the original ideas. They clarify language and review key vocabulary, they review the steps, they illuminate the meaning behind the concepts and skills, and they make the learning relevant by demonstrating applications.

Routinely Re-Teach

Great teachers routinely re-teach. Re-teaching is distinguished from reviewing in both substance and time involved. Re-teaching consists of another teaching round, in which the teacher differentiates the initial lesson and re-teaches the concepts and skills with an entirely different approach. Re-teaching is guaranteeing that the teacher offers another entry point for learners.

> **Re-teaching consists of another teaching round, in which the teacher differentiates the initial lesson and re-teaches the concepts and skills with an entirely different approach.**

According to Tomlinson (1999) , the reasons teachers must differentiate the lesson include three elements: learner readiness (ability), learner interests (choice), and learner profile (strengths and weaknesses). As the teacher re-teaches a lesson, he can differentiate by changing the content, the process or the product (Tomlinson, 1999; Fogarty & Pete, 2005).

By changing the content, the teacher offers different levels of complexity (concrete, representational, abstract), different resources (text, novel, web-site), and different learning environments (classroom, library, computer lab). For example, a re-teaching of states of matter may have students reading a selected text to reinforce the original hands-on learning where they experienced changing "states of matter" as they made pudding in the classroom.

By changing the process the teacher offers different instructional procedures: direct instruction (anticipatory set, input, guided practice, independent practice, assessment), co-operative learning (pairs, pairs of pairs), and inquiry modes (Problem-Based Learning, Case Studies, Service Learning). For example, as the teacher assigns the text in the re-teaching of states of matter, she may choose to use a co-operative jigsaw, in which four students are each assigned one part of the text to read and then share the information with the other team members.

By changing the product, teachers offer different entry points and exit or end points (eight multiple intelligences), and evidence of accountability (traditional assessments, portfolio assessments, performance assessments). For example, the teacher may re-teach the lesson on states of matter and offer students three options for follow-up to the lesson: do another hands on experiment with a partner (bodily/interpersonal), research the concept on the web (verbal/bodily), or write about the concept in their journals (verbal/intrapersonal).

They give more opportunity for the advanced learners for rapid pacing, challenge and enrichment through individual choice for independent endeavors.

When teachers differentiate a lesson, they not only give students optional ways to understand the concepts and skills, but they purposefully and intentionally give more time on task for the developing learner. At the same time, they give more opportunity for the advanced learners for rapid pacing, challenge and enrichment through individual choice for independent endeavors.

Routinely Revise

Great teachers routinely revise student learning during the teaching/learning cycle. They guide student thinking, or in the terminology of Feuerstein (1980), they mediate the learning with delving questions that help the student to sort out his thinking. According to Feuerstein (1980), the learning needs mediation to avoid misconceptions of misunderstandings. Simply put, Piaget (1954) postulates that the learners construct meaning in their minds. In fact, he is considered the Father of Constructivism.

Following the foundations of the constructivist model, Vygotsky (1978) comes along, and advocates a theory that says that not only do learners construct meaning in their minds, but they develop that meaning and understanding through interactions with others. In a social setting with colleagues, learners try out their ideas in dialogues and conversations. As they articulate their understandings, they are internalizing the deeper meaning in their minds.

Finally, Feuerstein builds on Piaget's and Vygotsky's theories and basically states that learners construct meaning in their minds, as Piaget says. Learners advance their ideas in social settings as they articulate their thoughts with others, as Vygotsky states. And, the learner learns with clarity and deep understanding through the mediation, the guidance, and the benefit of a teacher, parent, or peer. As the teacher or mediator intervenes with clarifying thoughts and questions, the learner revises his thinking to accommodate the theory correctly and carefully.

For example, mediating questions, much like Socratic dialogue, require more strategic thought by the learner as they define and limit the theory for accuracy (see Figure 7 below).

Why do you think that?

What is the supporting evidence for your thinking?

How might you demonstrate that?

Do you have a next step in mind?

Could you replicate that?

Figure 7 Mediating Questions

In addition to this explicit mediation of learning, there is another simple strategy that great teachers employ. They correct all answers so students are left with the right answer in their minds. They often go over test questions that stumped the students and clarify the response that is most appropriate, and why it is the best answer. By revising student thinking immediately, or as soon as is humanly possible, teachers take advantage of the teachable moments. The questions are still on the students minds and they are curious about the "right answer."

Routinely revising thinking, revising student answers, and revising learner understandings is a viable method used by quality teachers. In fact, as they revisit, review, re-teach, and revise, these teachers know that every kid is on board, because they leave nothing to chance.

Strategies

Revisit with a Two-Minute Buzz

Teachers revisit ideas introduced earlier by simply touching back to the key points throughout the day. They literally let the ideas spiral though the day, the week, the unit with frequent, constant, and brief reminders of the talking points: "Remember, there are eight parts of speech … see if you can name them to your partner in a 'two-minute buzz.' Now, let's see if we hit a homerun. Here are the eight: noun, verb, pronoun, adverb, adjective, preposition, conjunction, and interjection. Try it one more time."

Review by Dialing 4-1-1 and Connecting

The review lesson is a bit more specific and/or detailed. It is a more explicit check for understanding using two formats: Dial 4-1-1 for Information and Use the 3-2-1 Connect.

Dial 4-1-1 for Information.

Four target points—things specifically remembered from

the lesson (four of the simple machines: pulley, lever, wedge, wheel, ... and screw and inclined plane)

One peripheral learning—something not taught directly by the teacher, but learned by the student (how to use a memory cue to remember the simple machines: s-w-w-l-i-p)

One call to action—something the student is going to do (I'm going to look for simple machines in my house tonight.)

Use the 3-2-1 Connect

Kids dialogue with a partner on the following:
Three recalls or things they remember from the lesson ...
Two insights or connections they made ...
One question they may have ...

Re-teach the MI Way

Teachers routinely use 4–5 minute reviews using the multiple intelligences approach to differentiate the learning. Use the "V-V-I-I-M-M-N-B" acronym to remember the eight intelligences as depicted in Figure 8.

Verbal/Linguistic: reading, writing, speaking, listening

Visual/Spatial: drawing, sketching, graphic representations

Interpersonal/Social: leading, communicating, teaming, resolving conflicts

Intrapersonal/Introspective: reflecting

Mathematical/Logical: calculating, computing, reasoning

Musical/Rhythmic: performing, appreciating

Naturalist/Physical World: classifying flora, fauna and natural environment

Bodily/Kinesthetic: moving, doing, role-playing, building

Figure 8 Multiple Intelligences (MI)

If the teacher introduces the lesson through a verbal/linguistic (teacher-talk) and bodily/kinesthetic (hands-on) approach, they may re-teach the ideas through a micro-lesson using a visual/spatial approach (a chart or graphic organizer) to remind students of the key points.

Revise for Precision and Accuracy

A powerful and necessary strategy to close the achievement gap is for teachers to revise the responses and answers for the students so they leave the moment with the correct information, rather than misconceptions or misinformation. This revision is the teachable moment as mentioned earlier. Kids want to know the "right" answer when they are in the midst of working the problem. This is when they are most focused and motivated to learn. This is when the teacher mediates or guides the learning, correcting all wrong answers along the way.

Reflection

Invitation to Learn

There's a party in education and you're invited! An invitation is like a letter, it must be opened, read, and responded to. How will you respond? Will you say:

"What invitation?"
Never received the invitation; unaware; retired on the job ...

"I wasn't invited!"
"They're doing it to us" ... whoever they are and whatever it is; victim of the system ...

"I was invited, but I'm not going!"
Chooses not to participate; thinks the pendulum will swing back; the cynic ...

"I'm going!"
Preaching to the choir; you're here; the professional; quality matters to you ...

"I'm giving the party!"
Leaders; innovators; movers and shakers who care ...

Film

Teachers

This old film (1984) shows a scene in which a teacher dresses as Lincoln and recites the Gettysburg Address, and then dresses as Washington and simulates rowing across the Delaware. Use it to illustrate a teacher who leaves nothing to chance.

Chapter 5
Make No Excuses: Encourage At-Risk Participation

"What is it about me you can't teach? Is it that I am hearing impaired? Is it that I speak a different language? Is it because my parents don't come to conferences? Is it that I am a different color? Is it because I am ADD? Is it because I'm late for school? Is it because I learn more quickly than some? What is it about me you can't teach?"

–Eleanor Renee Rodriquez (1996)

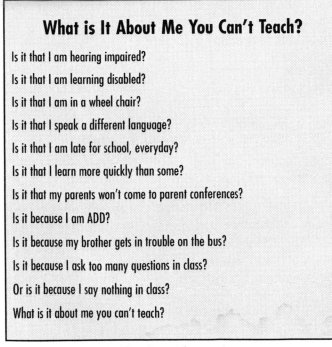

What is It About Me You Can't Teach?

Is it that I am hearing impaired?

Is it that I am learning disabled?

Is it that I am in a wheel chair?

Is it that I speak a different language?

Is it that I am late for school, everyday?

Is it that I learn more quickly than some?

Is it that my parents won't come to parent conferences?

Is it because I am ADD?

Is it because my brother gets in trouble on the bus?

Is it because I ask too many questions in class?

Or is it because I say nothing in class?

What is it about me you can't teach?

Figure 9 What Is It?

One of the most powerful strategies to close the achievement gap is the most basic and the most obvious of all teaching/learning strategies. It is the frequent, fluent, and full participation by all students. If learners are there, in the moment, ready, and willing to learn, the chances of them learning are increased greatly.

> **If learners are there, in the moment, ready, and willing to learn, the chances of them learning are increased greatly.**

To have students active, engaged, intensely involved; to have them interested, invested, and tuned-in to the learning, is the key to high achievement. Yet, it may be even more urgent for the reluctant, at-risk, academically challenged students that comprise the majority of achievement gap population.

Creating classrooms that invite active, engaged, and invested learners to own the learning is no small challenge for the classroom teacher of today. Given the dramatic demographics of minority populations, English language learners, low socio-economic status, high mobility rates, and a thousand other factors, teachers are hard-pressed to invite all learners to participate fully in the learning.

In addition to facing student's feelings of apathy and despair, of ignorance and ill-will, of low self-esteem and little self-confidence, teachers also must face their own feelings of dread and doubt. No matter how much they care or how much they try, many teachers feel that the situation in their school is hopeless for these youngsters. They feel like these kids are lost to, and in, the system. In fact, many of the reigning experts (Schmoker, 1996; Reeves, 2001; Marzano, 2001; Haycock, 2001) say that this is the most difficult issue in school reform: convincing teachers that they can, and do, make the difference.

To respond to the challenge, "What is it about me you can't teach?" the resounding answer is, "Nothing! There is nothing about you I can't teach. In fact, I believe that I can teach any kid anything. I am a master teacher. I have a vast repertoire of instructional tools to work with as I craft the learning for a diverse set of learners. Among my most valued are four tools of choice:

1) Active Learning

2) Mindful Engagement

3) Intense Involvement

4) Invested Stakeholders."

Active Learning

Co-operative Learning

Active learning strategies include the essential repertoire of co-operative learning, a multiple intelligences approach, and higher order thinking skills. To be considered part of the team, to have roles and responsibilities, and to belong to the group, is what co-operative learning is all about. Active learning is the hallmark of these co-operative interactions.

Multiple Intelligences

An MI approach targets the many intelligences of every child. It is the key to differentiation, allowing different entry points and end points for the learner. In an MI classroom, kids believe they can learn.

Higher Order Thinking

HOT challenges kids to think, to make decisions, and to and solve problems. It leaves kids wanting more than just the tip of the iceberg. They want alternatives, solutions, closure to the conundrums they are tackling. HOT is what hooks kids into real, in-depth learning.

Mindful Engagement

Solitary Endeavors

Unlike active learning models, mindful engagement is often a solitary endeavor in which the learner searches for meaning in a very personal way. This is the moment in the teaching/learning cycle that is highly reflective. It is when the learner connects the new learning to existing schema in the mind. Since each learner has an entirely different set of schema or background knowledge, it follows that each person makes meaning of things in his/her own way. It is in this reflective mode that the learner develops a deeper understanding of new, incoming information.

> **Since each learner has an entirely different set of schema or background knowledge, it follows that each person makes meaning of things in his/her own way.**

Team Efforts

Mindful engagement is often a by-product of the active learning segments. As learners become actively committed to the co-operative task, they begin to explore, examine, and extrapolate ideas that fit with the learning and with their own understandings and previously held concepts. In fact, this is part of the process of developing new concepts. It is in the quiet time following the activity that the brain begins to make sense of what is going on. It is through deep processing of the information and data that the brain makes critical connections and begins to "understand."

Intense Involvement

Highly Focused

"Highly focused," "persistent," and even "tenacious" are words that define this state of intense involvement. It is a level of concentration that defies interruption. Learners are barely aware that someone has spoken to them or is attempting to get their attention.

Flow

Csikszentmihalyi describes this intense involvement as the state of "flow." This state when the learner has a level of expertise that allows him/her to enter into a state of awareness, of an intense enjoyment, of time passing without noticing.

Invested Stakeholders

Relevance

Relevance is the key to authentic learning and the stakeholder role in Problem-Based Learning creates a relevance for the learner. They become part of the scenario and they see the solution as a personal victory.

Point of View

When learners take on a point of view, they have a built-in bias that causes emotional involvement and real investment of time, energy, and emotion. The students work from a particular point of view that is key to the

When learners take on a point of view, they have a built-in bias that causes emotional involvement and real investment of time, energy, and emotion.

investment of the learners. They own the problem because they have a stake in it.

Strategies

Fishbowl, Card Game, and TAG

Teachers who are aware of the achievement gap and its implications strive to call on kids randomly, or with the help of a "random" system, to ensure that all students have equal opportunity to respond. Teachers may call on students using a fishbowl of names (Bell, 2002), a deck of cards (that has a corresponding deck passed out to students as the enter the room), or by using the TAG strategy in which a small group of kids are to TAG "Talk Around the Group" by passing an object to the next person in the group.

Co-operative Learning Strategies

Many teachers use co-operative learning strategies and structures (Johnson, Johnson, & Holubec, 1986) to facilitate learning. This kind of interaction effort encourages participation by all students, especially those at-risk students who may be least willing to talk in class. Some of the most common strategies are listed in Figure 10.

Whole Group Strategies

Whole group strategies and structures include: the People Search, the Human Graph, and the Three Musketeers.

Whole Group Strategies

People Search (Fogarty & Bellanca, 1990)

Human Graph (Fogarty & Bellanca, 1990)

Three Musketeers (Kagan, 1986)

Partner Strategies

2-4-8 (Fogarty & Bellanca, 1990)

TTYPA ... Tell and Retell (Fogarty, 1990)

Think/Pair/Share (Lyman & McTighe, 1988)

Figure 10 Co-operative Learning Strategies

The People Search

Prepared by the teacher, prior to the kids arriving, The People Search asks kids to: "Find someone who ..."

While this is frequently used as an ice-breaker, its greater value is as a learning tool. Use before the lesson, it allows students to interact and stir up prior knowledge about a topic. Used after the lesson, it allows students to revisit and review ides from the lesson. Usually there are between 5–10 statements for students such as: "Find someone who ... can predict what the story is about."

The Human Graph

The Human Graph is exactly that. It requires kids to stand along a continuum based on their opinion of a given statement and physically form a graph of human beings. For example, for a question such as "The legislative branch is the most important branch of the government" students would stand a long a continuum that runs from "Agree" to "Disagree" and be ready to justify their stance.

The Three Musketeers

Three students are required to meet and discuss a specified topic. The team then reports back a summary statement. For example, "Tell three ways you used data today."

Partner Strategies

Partner interactions include: the 2-4-8 Focus Interview, TTYPA ..., and Think/Pair/Share.

2-4-8 Focus Interview

In this activity students should tell three stories, each one different from the last:

Two kids begin by sharing an artifact of their work (for example, a book report).

Four kids meet as a pair of pairs and retell their partner's stories.

Eight kids meet, 2 sets of 4, and each tells a story from the previous group of 4.

TTYPA ...

A simple strategy that calls on students to Turn To Your Partner And ... discuss an assigned topic or idea. It's an informal interaction that gets kids to connect to the lecture or the learning.

Think/Pair/Share

A more formal interaction, students are required to think on their own and then to pair up with a partner and come up with a shared answer.

Reflection

Teachers that take the time and the effort to encourage all kids, to compliment all kids, and to say those words that stay with a kid the rest of his life, are the teachers who understand that the achievement gap affects the entire child, not just his academic standing.

"You're a hero to someone ... act like the hero you are!" is an example of one of those memorable moments when the teacher says something profound and lasting for some kid who needs that energy and encouragement at that very moment.

Film

Mr. Holland's Opus

Scene from Mr. Holland's Opus (1995): The Coach and Mr. Holland, the band instructor, are seated on the front porch, playing a game of chess.

> Coach: (to Mr. Holland) You mean you have a willing kid, and you can't teach him how to bang a drum? Then, you're not a very good teacher.

Chapter 6
Insist on Results: Emphasize Reading

"When kids can't, won't, or don't read, nothing else matters. It affects everything else they do in school and beyond."

Fogarty

Much of the introductory material in this discussion on the achievement gap deals with the concept of literacy. Astonishing statistics are cited and the case is made that literacy is at the root of the gap challenge. Literacy is what sets us apart from other species. It's what the human race is about. After all, literacy is what makes us intellectually able to move about the world. It is about creative ideation, productive problem solving, and mindful decision-making. Literacy is the gift of communication, articulation, and pontification.

According to some experts, it is the right of every child in the classroom to have quality teaching that gives all children the gift of literacy (Haycock, 2001) If that is so, then, as Bell (2002) advocates, to ensure the literacy skills of every child in every classroom, teachers must first and foremost embrace the reading program in their school.

Whether they like it or not, does not matter. Whatever the existing reading program in the school is, it must have the full support, complete understanding, and earnest effort of every single teacher on the faculty. Is it not a choice item. It is the reading right of the every individual student in that school. And, it is the responsibility, the obligation, the mandate, if you will, of every last teacher to embrace the reading program with sincerity and with integrity.

To embrace the reading program means lots of different things. It means understanding and using the materials and supporting the published texts, workbooks, and literary selections provided, with supplemental resources that are appropriate and available. Embracing the reading program means developing a robust and print-rich environment in the classroom and it means designing reading instruction and interventions that get measurable results in terms of reading ability and reading versatility.

> **It is the responsibility, the obligation, the mandate, if you will, of every last teacher to embrace the reading program with sincerity and with integrity.**

Understanding and Using the Published Materials

It is necessary to understand and use materials provided by the district for reading instruction if teachers are to fully accept the reading program that is selected. It means that teachers work in skillful and effective ways with the texts, the workbooks, the worksheets, the tests, and supplemental material provided. They incorporate the skills and concepts of the program, with an understanding of the scope and sequence outlined by the publisher. Yet, professional teachers also, modify and adjust the instructional program as they go to fit the needs of their particular students.

They use the materials in meaningful learning experiences as the students proceed through a comprehensive instructional reading program. In fact, that is the most compelling reason for teachers to embrace the selected program, whether they "like" it or not. The school reading program is comprehensive in scope, systematically introducing a set of skills that build upon each other. It is this systematic approach that offers the most hope for reading instruction, just as it does for other kinds of subject matter instruction, including math, science, music, and just about any discipline you can imagine.

Now, that doesn't mean that the teachers use the material as a "plug and play" program. It means just the opposite. Skillful teachers use the published reading program as their home base. They play by the rules of the game, always with their eye on the ball. Yet, they utilize the expertise of skillful coaches as they check their playbook for the appropriate calls. Quality teachers know the rules of the game, they see the big picture, and they understand exactly what the goal is, at all times. But they also realize that they must put their touch on the game to get the most from the players they know so well.

> **Quality teachers know the rules of the game, they see the big picture, and they understand exactly what the goal is, at all times.**

Providing Supplemental Resources

Providing resources that are appropriate, available, and supportive of the school reading program is what quality teachers do, as they masterfully work with the district-approved reading program. Quality-minded teachers bring a wealth of additional resources to the instructional scene. These resources span the spectrum from actual reading materials from former or other programs, to literature selections that are perfectly suited to the theme, to activities that scaffold the targeted skills, to on-line selections that dove-tail with the instruction.

The idea of using materials from other programs is really only natural for seasoned staff. Often, they have used another program for a number of years and they have developed rich instructional activities that they know work. The only caveat is that these materials be used as additional resources, not as the centerpiece of the instruction.

At the same time, teachers may include literature pieces that enhance the district program. Again, there is much wonderful and worthy literature that easily accompanies any reading program. Yet, caution is again signaled, to use this other literature to complement the actual published materials and recommended literature, not to replace it. Of course, the same is true of the activities that seem to fit. Quality teachers use them with care, carefully weaving them into the current reading curriculum

Developing a Print-Rich Environment that is both Rich and Robust

Another dimension of the literacy focus is a print-rich environment that suggests a wide variety of reading materials and innumerable opportunities for writing. These include both fiction and non-fiction materials that span the spectrum from picture books and poetry anthologies, to newspapers and magazines. It includes writing centers, writing materials, and reasons for writing that range from invitations and announcements, to summaries and reports.

They know that print, in reading, or in writing prevail in the classroom.

A print-rich environment that is robust, is steaming with a versatile repertoire of reading matter that is easily accessible and always available to the youngsters in that classroom. The kids see, taste, touch, smell, and feel the print in any and every form possible. They know that print, in reading, or in writing, prevails in the classroom. They see examples of primary documents such as the Declaration of Independence and they see business letters, authentic journals, travel diaries, and posted notices. The kids realize that print is there to be read and print is there to be written.

Designing Reading Instruction and Interventions for Results

Rather than simply going through the motions of the reading instruction program, to get to the heart of the "literacy gap" the quality teacher puts all the pieces together and creates a seamless program for all levels. These teachers smooth out the various chunks of the program and understand when to go wide and when to go deep.

These quality teachers are astute diagnosticians. They know how to observe, how to assess, and how to draw conclusions about students' abilities, their strengths and weaknesses, their mastery of certain skills, and their needs for development of other skills. These excellent teachers know what they see, and they know how to prescribe interventions according to the evidence available. They know how to read achievement data from the state, from their own tests and quizzes, and from students' daily work. And they know when and how to determine appropriate literacy and learning interventions that get results.

■ ☐ ■ ☐ ■

In addition, teachers that are exceptionally skillful in their work, teachers who know how to motivate and excite their students with learning, teachers who accept nothing but success for all, incite their students toward versatile kinds of reading and writing. They foster flexible reading that takes students toward multiple genres so they can explore and examine the full range of reading materials.

These are the teachers who help kids find the "kind of books" they each prefer. These teachers lead students to a variety of journals, magazines, and newspapers so that students eventually find reading materials that appeal to them. Students who are required to read widely find their favorite authors and their favorite genre because they have been exposed repeatedly to so many choices.

When teachers embrace the reading program, they have a comprehensive and systemic scope and sequence of skills.

When teachers embrace the reading program, they have a comprehensive and systemic scope and sequence of skills. At the same time, they have the opportunity to enhance the approved program with their expertise. This comprises literacy instruction that taps into both the science and the art of quality teaching.

Strategies

Learning to Read

One way to embrace the school reading program is to use the materials that are supplies. To begin with, teachers might want to think about how they themselves learned to read. They might want to think about their earliest memory of learning to read. Was it Sally, Dick, and Jane books?

Phonics? Being read to? Or, just learning to say the words as you looked through a book. Once teachers think about how their own reading journey began, they might want to ask students the similar questions:

How did you learn to read?

What is your earliest memory of learning to read?

Are you a good reader today? How do you know?

Loving to Read

Teachers model the love of reading by reading at the start of each day, by reading at the end of each day, and by reading during transitions throughout the day. A great book with little snippets to read all day long is *Where the Sidewalk Ends* by Shel Silverstein (1974).

Getting Kids to Love to Read

Teachers can read aloud, or have kids read, books about school. See Figure 11 for some great picture books that all kids, of all ages, relate to.

Thank-You, Mr. Falkner by Patricia Polacco

Leo, the Late Bloomer by Robert Kraus

Testing Miss Malarky by Judy Finchler

Harold and the Purple Crayon by Crockett Johnson

Through the Cracks by Carolyn Sollman

Figure 11 Motivational Books about School

Self-Selected Reading

Two strategies that motivate kids to read self-selected material include Sustained Silent Reading (Trelease 2001) and Literature Circles (Cunningham 2000). In both situations students decide on the book they will read. In the Sustained Silent Reading (SSR) situation, they read on their own for extended periods of time with a book that is at their level and of high interest to them.

With the process called, Literature Circles, the students take on various roles:

Literary Luminary—reads favorite passages.

Discussion Leader—develops critical questions.

Illustrator—creates cover art for book.

Word Wizard—finds 3–5 vocabulary words of interest.

Within this structure, the group reads assigned sections and then comes prepared to participate with the various activities.

Vocabulary Building

There are four ways listed here to build vocabulary, although there are many more.

The four ways to build vocabulary include the 4-Fold Concept, ABC Graffiti, White Out, and the Prefix Pocket Guide.

Vocabulary—4-Fold (Fogarty)

Working in groups, and using large poster paper, students fold the paper into four corner sections, labeling as follows and doing the instructions as given. Select a target word: democracy, agriculture, reformation ...

Top left: LIST *10–20 Synonyms*	Top right: RANK *Prioritize the top 3*
Bottom left: COMPARE *(Target word) is like (concrete object) because both ...*	Bottom right: ILLUSTRATE *Draw a visual metaphor*

ABC Graffiti

Use the entire alphabet to spark words beginning with every letter to explain or describe an idea, object or event. For example: "parachute"

A—Airy

B—Big

C—Colorful

D—Dangerous

E—Earth-bound, etc.

White Out

Create a list of vocabulary words on the computer, enlarge the font, and then print out the list. Once printed, use thin "white out" tape and tape through the center of each word. Make copies and have students identify the words.

Prefix Pocket Guide

Using 10–15 key prefixes, have students create a little booklet of words that begin with the various prefixes. For example, page 1: dis- (discouraged, dismiss, disembark, etc.).

Comprehension Strategies

One of the most popular and practical little book is entitled *Mosaic of Thought,* by Keene and Zimmerman (1997). In this book, the authors identify seven keys to comprehension, as depicted in Figure 12. Have the students work with these keys by making a journal or chart to reference when they are reading.

1. Stir Up Prior Knowledge
2. Synthesize and Summarize
3. Ask Questions
4. Find Important Themes
5. Make Inferences
6. Visualize
7. Use "Fix-up" Strategies

Figure 12 Comprehension Strategies

Delve into Data

Strategies to close the achievement gap must include data. Teachers are encouraged to look over their test data, work samples, and observational data to determine the most powerful instructional strategies to target for improvement. Using the four questions listed in Figure 13, teachers can begin to gather, analyze, and interpret data for instructional purposes.

What data do we have?

What else do we know or need to know?

So, what does the data mean? What can we conclude or infer?

Now, what do we need to do?

Figure 13 Data Questions to Ask

Reflection

Let the data tell the story of achievement.

Trust the data you have ... it's all you have right now.

Don't let the data monopolize the conversations. Get to the solutions; the interventions!

Focus on results: quick results, visible results, reliable results!

Films

Pay It Forward

Kevin Spacey's opening welcome to Middle School, for his 7th grade class in this epic film from 2000:

"What does the world expect of you? What if you don't like the world the way it is?

I will be here for you. I expect you to be here for me.

You will learn to love words in this class. If you don't know a word, you will look it up."

References

Bell, L. (2002, Dec.) Strategies to close the achievement gap. *Educational Leadership*. Association for Supervision and Curriculum Development.

Bloom, B. S., Engelhart, M. S., Furst, E. J., Hill, W. H., & Krathwohl, D. R. (1956). *Taxonomy of educational objectives: Cognitive domain, Handbook 1*. New York: David McKay Co.

Caine, G., Caine, R. N., & Crowell, S. (1999). *Mindshifts: A brain-compatible process for professional development and the renewal of education* (2nd edn). Tucson, AZ: Zephyr Press.

Caine, R. N., & Caine, G. (1991). *Making connections: Teaching and the human brain*. Alexandria, VA: Association for Supervision and Curriculum Development.

Caine, R. N., & Caine, G. (1994). *Making connections: Teaching and the human brain*. New York: Innovative Learning Publications, Addison-Wesley Publishing.

Coleman, J.S., et al. (1986). *Equality of educational opportunity*. Washington, DC: Office of Education.

Dead Poets Society (1989) motion picture. Directed by Peter Weir. Touchstone Pictures, USA.

Edmonds, Ronald R. (1979). "Some Schools Work and More Can" *Social Policy*, March/April, p. 28–32.

Edmonds, Ronald R. (1981). "*Making Public Schools Effective.*" *Social Policy*. September/October, p56–60.

Feuerstein, R. (1980). *Instrumental enrichment*. Baltimore: University Park Press.

Fogarty, R., & Pete, B. (2004). *A look at transfer: Seven strategies that work*. Chicago: Fogarty & Associates.

Fogarty, R. (1997). *Brain compatible classrooms*. Arlington Heights, IL: Skylight Training and Publishing.

Fogarty, R. (2001). *Differentiated learning: Different strokes for different folks.* Chicago: Fogarty & Associates.

Fogarty, R. (2002) *Making sense of the research on the brain and learning.* Chicago: Fogarty & Associates.

Fogarty, R. (2001). *Student learning standards: A blessing in disguise.* Chicago: Fogarty & Associates.

Fogarty, R. (2001). *Teachers make a the difference: A framework for quality.* Chicago: Fogarty & Associates.

Goleman, D. (1995). *Emotional intelligence: Why it can matter more than IQ.* New York: Bantam Books.

Gardner, H. (1983). *Frames of mind: The theory of multiple intelligences.* New York: Basic Books.

Gardner, H. (1999). *Intelligence reframed: Multiple intelligences for the 21st century.* New York: Basic Books.

Haycock, K. (2001). Closing the achievement gap. *Educational Leadership.* Alexandria, VA: Association for Supervision and Curriculum Development. 58(6),6–11.

Holmes, O.W. (1939). *Poet at the breakfast table.* Haughton Mifflin, Boston.

Hunter, M. (1971). *Transfer.* El Segundo, CA: TIP Publications.

Johnson, D. W., Johnson, R. T., & Holubec, E. J. (1986). *Circles of learning: Cooperation in the classroom.* Alexandria, VA: Association for Supervision and Curriculum Development.

Joyce, B. R., & Showers, B. (1983). *Power in staff development through research and training.* Alexandria, VA: Association for Supervision and Curriculum Development.

Joyce, B., & Showers, B. (1995). *Student achievement through staff development* (2nd edn). White Plains, NY: Longman.

Kagan, S. (1989). Cooperation works! *Educational Leadership, 47*(4), 12–15.

Keene, E.O., Zimmerman S. (1997). *Mosaic of thought.* Portsmouth, NH: Heinemann

Kerman, K. (1982). *Teacher Expectations, Student Achievement. (TESA)* Los Angeles County Board of Education.

Kohn, A. (1993). *Punished by rewards.* New York: Houghton Mifflin.

Lyman, F., & McTighe, J. (1988). Cueing thinking in the classroom: The promise of theory-embedded tools. *Educational Leadership, 45(7)*, 18–24.

Marzano, R. (2004). *Building background knowledge.* Alexandria, VA: Association for Supervision and Curriculum Development.

Marzano, R., Norford, J., Paynter, D., Pickering, D., & Gaddy, B. (2001). *A handbook for classroom instruction that works.* Alexandria, VA: Association for Supervision and Curriculum Development.

Marzano, R., Pickering, D., & Pollock J. (2001). *Classroom instruction that works: Research-based strategies for increasing student achievement.* Alexandria, VA: Association for Supervision and Curriculum Development.

Mr. Holland's Opus (1995) motion picture. Directed by Stephen Herek. Hollywood Pictures, USA.

Pay It Forward (2000) motion picture. Directed by Mimi Leder. Warner Brothers, USA.

Pete, B., & Fogarty, R. J. (2003). *Twelve brain principles that make the difference.* Chicago: Fogarty & Associates.

Pete, B. and R. Fogarty. (2005). *Closing the achievement gap: Strategies that work.* Chicago, IL: Robin Fogarty & Associates, Ltd.

Piaget, J. (1954). *The construction of reality in the child.* New York: Basic Books.

Reeves, D. (2001). *Accountability In action: A summary of the work developed by Doug Reeves.* CO: <www.makingstandardswork.com>

Robinson, F. P. (1970). *Effective study.* New York: Harper & Row.

Rodriquez, E. (1996). *What is it about me you can't teach?* Arlington Heights, IL: Skylight Training and Publishing.

Rowe, M. B. (1974). Wait time and rewards as instructional variables, their influence on language, logic and fate control: part 1. Wait-time. *Journal of Research in Science Teaching, 11*, 81–94.

Saturday Night Live: The best of Jerry Seinfield (1992) television program. Starring Jerry Seinfield. Broadway Video, New York.

Schmoker, M. (1996). *Results: The key to continuous school improvement.* Alexandria, VA: Association for Supervision and Curriculum Development.

Silverstein, S. (1974). *Where the sidewalk ends.* New York: Harper and Row.

Sollman, C. (1994). *Through the cracks.* Worcester, MA: Davis Publications.

Sousa, D. (1995). *How the brain learns: A classroom teacher's guide.* Reston, VA: The National Association of Secondary Schools.

Sprenger, M. (1999). *Learning and memory: The brain in action.* Alexandria, VA: Association for Supervision and Curriculum Development.

Stanovitch, K.E. (1986) Mathew effects in reading: Same consequences of individual differences in acquisition of literacy. *Reading Research Quarterly. 21*(4): 360–406.

Stronge, J. (2002). *Qualities of effective teachers.* Alexandria, VA: Association for Supervision and Curriculum Development.

Teachers (1984) motion picture. Directed by Arthur Hiller. MGM Studio, USA.

To Sir, With Love (1967) motion picture. Directed by James Clavell. Columbia Pictures, USA.

Vacca, R. T. (2002). From efficient decoders to strategic readers. *Educational Leadership, 60*(3), 6–11.

Vygotsky, L. (1978). *Mind in society. Cambridge,* MA: Harvard University Press.

Walberg, H. J. (1999). Productive teaching. In H.C. Waxman & H. J. Walberg (Eds.), *New directions for teaching practice and research* (pp. 75–104). Berkeley, CA: McCutchen Publishing.

Bibliography

Ausubel, D. (1978). *Educational psychology: A cognitive view* (2nd edn). New York: Holt, Rinehart, & Winston.

Bruer, J. (1999). *Myth of the first three years: A new understanding of early brain development and lifelong learning.* New York: The Free Press.

Cooney, W. C., Cross, B., & Trunk, B. (1993). *From Plato to Piaget: The greatest theorists from across the centuries and around the world.* New York: University Press of America.

D'Arcangelo, M. (2000). The scientist in the crib: A conversation with Andrew Meltzoff. *Educational Leadership, 58(3),* 8–13.

Deming, W. E. (1986). *Out of the crisis.* Cambridge, MA: The MIT Press.

Diamond, M., & Hobson, J. (1998). *Magic trees of the mind: How to nurture your child's intelligence, creativity, and healthy emotions from birth to adolescence.* New York: Dutton.

Eisner, E. (1979). *The educational imagination: On the design and evaluation of school programs.* New York: Macmillan Publishing.

Fogarty, R. (1997). *Brain compatible classrooms.* Arlington Heights, IL: Skylight Training and Publishing.

Fogarty, R. (2001). *Differentiated learning: Different strokes for different folks.* Chicago: Fogarty & Associates.

Fogarty, R. (2002) *Making sense of the research on the brain and learning.* Chicago: Fogarty & Associates.

Fogarty, R. (2001). *Student learning standards: A blessing in disguise.* Chicago: Fogarty & Associates.

Fogarty, R. (2001). *Teachers make a the difference: A framework for quality.* Chicago: Fogarty & Associates.

Gopnik, A., Meltzoff, A., & Kuhl, P. (1999). *The scientist in the crib: Minds, brains, and how children learn.* New York: William Morrow.

Hannaford, C. (1995). *Smart moves: Why learning is not all in your head.* Arlington, VA: Great Ocean Publishers.

Hart, L. (1983). *Human brain, human learning.* Kent, WA: Books for Educators.

Hyerle, D. (1996). *Visual tools for constructing knowledge.* Alexandria, VA: Association for Supervision and Curriculum Development.

Jensen, E. (1996). *Brain-based learning.* Del Mar, CA: Turning Point Publishing.

Jensen, E. (1999). *Teaching with the brain in mind.* Alexandria, VA: Association for Supervision and Curriculum Development.

Jensen, E. (2000). *Moving with the brain in mind.* Educational Leadership 58(3), 34–37.

Kotulak, R. (1996). *Inside the brain: Revolutionary discoveries of how the mind works.* Kansas City, KS: Andrews and McMeel.

La Doux, J. (1996). *The emotional brain: The mysterious underpinnings of emotional life.* New York: Simon and Schuster.

Mangan, M. (1998). *Brain compatible science.* Arlington Heights, IL: Skylight Training and Publishing.

Marzano, R. (2004) *Building background knowledge.* Alexandria, VA: Association for Supervision and Curriculum Development.

Marzano, R., Norford, J., Paynter, D., Pickering, D., & Gaddy, B. (2001). *A handbook for classroom instruction that works.* Alexandria, VA: Association for Supervision and Curriculum Development.

Miles, M., & Hubberman, A. B. (1984). *Qualitative data analysis: A sourcebook of new methods.* Beverly Hills, CA: Sage.

Pinker, S. (1997). *How the mind works*. New York: W.W. Norton.

Robinson, F. P. (1970). *Effective study*. New York: Harper & Row.

Rowe, M. B. (1974). Wait time and rewards as instructional variables, their influence on language, logic and fate control: part 1. Wait-time. *Journal of Research in Science Teaching, 11*, 81–94.

Sousa, D. (1995). *How the brain learns: A classroom teacher's guide*. Reston, VA: The National Association of Secondary Schools.

Sprenger, M. (1999). *Learning and memory: The brain in action*. Alexandria, VA: Association for Supervision and Curriculum Development.

Sylwester, R. (1995). *Celebration of neurons: An educator's guide to the human brain*. Alexandria, VA: Association for Supervision and Curriculum Development.

Sylwester, R. (1998). *Student brains, school issues*. Arlington Heights, IL: Skylight Training and Publishing.

Sylwester, R. (2000). Unconscious emotions, conscious feelings. *Educational Leadership, 58(3)*, 20–24.

Westwater, A., & Wolfe, P. (2000). The brain compatible curriculum. *Educational Leadership, 58(3)*, 49–52.

Wolfe, P. (2000). *Brain matters*. Alexandria, VA: Association for Supervision and Curriculum Development.

Teachers Make ✗ the Difference

The good teacher *instructs,*
the excellent teacher *invites,*
the superior teacher *involves,*
the great teacher *inspires.*

Robin Fogarty—Chicago, 1999